The Hero's Brave Decisions

The Best Brave Thoughts

By

Bernard Benson Sarfo

The Hero's Brave Decisions

Bernard Benson Sarfo

Published by Bernard Benson Sarfo, 2024.

COPYRIGHT © 2024 BERNARD BENSON SARFO

All rights reserved. No part of this publication may be reproduced, stored in retrieval systems or transmitted in any form or by any means without prior written permission of the publisher. The only exception is brief quotation(s) in printed reviews and research works.

While every precaution has been taken in the preparation of this book, the publisher assumes no responsibility for errors or omissions, or for damages resulting from the use of the information contained herein.

THE HERO'S BRAVE DECISIONS

First edition. February 22, 2024.

Copyright © 2024 Bernard Benson Sarfo.

ISBN: 979-8224000319

Written by Bernard Benson Sarfo.

Also by Bernard Benson Sarfo

The Fact Among Facts (1st)
The Fact Among Facts

Standalone
The Youth Murderer
Be Original Not a Copy
The Christians Science or Scholarship
Precious than Paradise
Habit makes future
A shelter from storm and rain
The Science of Life
The Strongest Lion Knockback
The Perfect and Inspiring City
Above Hope, Faith and Love
The Hero's Brave Decisions
The Weakest Among Plants
The Hero's Brave Decisions

DEDICATION

I dedicate this book to everyone out there and wish them all the best!

DEDICATION

I dedicate this book to everyone out there and wish them all the best!

'When wisdom entered into your heart, and knowledge is pleasant unto your soul, discretion shall preserve you, understanding shall keep you' (Prov.2:10, 11).

INTRODUCTION

The world has so many lessons about lives and it results. The lessons comprise good, bad, bitter and so on. There are laws governing these existences and the fruit that bears shows the life starting point.

Carefulness, self-control and integrity are the foundation of natural life and those who consider and build the life on this foundation proof the secure life.

God created this world for a purpose and those who live on this world must live with the purpose. Without that, the life will be fruitless and is up to each one to choose for the outcome.

Life ever live as a uniqueness or profitable is by considering God who created the heaven and earth and there is no other thing else.

A good manager considers the right of the owner and make the good use of the things he or she manages. His idea as a manager identifies the peak of that knowledge apply and earns the best reward.

If God be your first consideration; then all things will work together for your best. The Life worthy to be praise is life that harvest God as the fruit and the only fruit that give life eternal is the body of Christ.

John 6:56-60 New International Version (NIV) 56 Whoever eats my flesh and drinks my blood remains in me, and I in them.

57 Just as the living Father sent me and I live because of the Father, so the one who feeds on me will live because of me.

58 This is the bread that came down from heaven. Your ancestors ate manna and died, but whoever feeds on this bread will live forever."

Every human being in this world ought to prepare to face the practical realities of life in this world – the opportunities, defeats, duties and the successes.

Life, as we may know, is not about bragging; but it involves preparation, planning, determination, activity, gentleness, integrity, pure thought, choice and the willingness.

Everything we do turns to us either for good or bad. A Life is like a tree; it bears fruit.

What you sow is what you reap. So the life that has hope stands only on Christ. Men! What is it about your life? Everyone has a tool that benefit him or she about his or her life journey.

This book will let us know more about the witness concerns heroism and their treatment in life and why they are hero's? What makes the hero or who is the hero?

Contents

1. Consider Your Acts

In life what you study becomes your behaviour. And how you behave is what teaches you. Sound comes by attack and there is no breath without air.

What you do whether good or bad resulted by your will. Your demand classifies you and proofs your being. You become what you study.

How you behave becomes part of you, and that is your character. What you always do is what you always know, and what you know becomes your understanding of what you do. What you always do indwells you, and what indwells you is the fruit you bear.

Your conduct bring blessing or curse into your life. Your attitude makes your wealth, whilst your bad ones are wrecks, and that is your reward.

You must be careful with how you behave, for that brings your blessing or curse. Your behaviour identifies you as a person, and that presents you to others. Your presentation becomes your personality.

Practice what is good and you will be good. You become a master by starting as a servant through practice.

Practice brings lessons, and these lessons bring studies. Studies bring creativity and creativity brings wealth.

You must be careful with what you bring out, for that leads to your success or failure. Let's consider what is best, pure and the truth, then we will not flop.

The Real life or natural life requires management and the good result of life stands on carefulness.

The Fruit of life centered on continue practice and the practice must be attitude and the attitude makes the reward of that life being setup whether good or bad.

In life, some people want to get everything on a silver platter rather than use accepted laws and regulations.

So many people take things for granted. Taking precautions prevents an accident, and it helps to do right things. Some people don't think before they act; rather, they act before they think.

Life can be sweet by carefulness and determination. And proper attention is the key that reveals knowledge and understanding.

Carefulness brings good wealth and gives a profit even to the foolish. Having a fresh thing with a fresh mind is better than an old thing used by an unknown person.

A new experience brings new knowledge; new knowledge brings research; and research brings a broad knowledge and understanding. A fresh husband is better than an old husband who wants to become fresh.

Almost always, we make mistakes in the things we do. Sometimes, we do things hastily without considering what the outcome would be.

We always pack up before thinking. But profit comes by carefulness of doing things. Never fail to plan; if you do, you have planned to fail. Life must be manage well.

2. Use The Opportunity Well

Master yourself as you want it and practice as you eat every day. Prepare yourself every moment and be ready for whatever comes.

Get ready for heat and never afraid to walk in the muddy and the snow. Raise your head up when there is a strong wind; means ever lose your chance because of trouble; be head on and take your price.

Never waste time when you have a chance to do something. Do what you can every moment and never stop progressing. Always enhance your knowledge if possible. Never give up, no matter the circumstance; press on to higher heights.

Life is hard, but it's better when you have what you need. Time is life, and the life is time; never joke with your time; do good things if you have time.

Seek other opportunities which can bring you wealth. Too much work can destroy but too much idleness leads to poverty. Do enough work but don't overwork.

Be faithful in your work; do not slack in any way. You will have what you need by working hard, and your reward will be full. Always learn good things and practise them. Never leave your good deeds; be a good example to others.

God has given us the chance to know him, who created heaven and earth. And this opportunity is your reward for you to know who God is.

Sometimes, circumstances in life which you think are your end are a tool for your victory and to help draw you closer to God.

Never think of lost because of the poor situation you find yourself in. The condition is there for only a moment; it will not be there to the end of your lifespan.

In life, sometimes, light becomes darkness for you, and you wouldn't know what to do or where to go.

Sometimes, you feel dead even though you are still living; life seems hopeless to you. Life becomes very difficult; people live on survival skills. Happiness becomes sorrow and mourning.

In times like these, never let hardship put you down or discourage you. Every man or woman born into this world is already victorious because of the opportunity to live.Never be discouraged, because of the hardship you are going through.

Exercise faith in God and be hopeful till the end. Hard times are opportunity days to discover your real being and your destiny. Never doubt God because of hard times.

In life, hard times teach us lessons of bitterness and the carefulness we should know for our progress.

We must accept every condition we are in and manage it well. Never announce your condition or make a noise of your situation.

All our conditions are aspects of our life's progress and benefits in every situation. In this world, every life has its record and reward. The lives we live cannot be equal; so are the situations we are passing through. Every life has its unique ways and conditions that one must pass through.

Never think you are cursed because of the hardship you are going through. Sometimes, life becomes unbearable but do not think it is a curse.

You may even prefer dying to living. You dislike existence in its entirety. But never kill yourself; look up to God for a breakthrough, and good things will happen to you.

Life can be sweet by carefulness and determination. And proper attention is the key that reveals knowledge and understanding. Carefulness brings good wealth and gives a profit even to the foolish.

Having a fresh thing with a fresh mind is better than an old thing used by an unknown person.

A new experience brings new knowledge; new knowledge brings research; and research brings a broad knowledge and understanding. A fresh husband is better than an old husband who wants to become fresh.

Life is about actions and inactions. But life's prosperity stands on choices. Never be down-spirited because of hardship; be courageous and move forward.

All people may be against you but you will be successful. The waves of life are inevitable. Sometimes, life can seem hopeless and dark as if you will not be successful. But be hopeful and courageous; never let it go.

Have faith in God and hold on to the end. Things will be better and profitable. Let your desire to succeed guide you to press even harder when things are tough. Discover what you need by searching deep. Discuss, work it out and hold on to the end.

Never abuse your dignity or throw out your inner beauty because of your hard situation. Let your hope be in God and be of good courage. Move and never return to Egypt for help.

3. Set The Right Purpose

Every life must have a purpose. Life without purpose ends in vanity. In life, one must have an aim to guide him to make the right choices.

Doing this consistently means that one has a vision. The end of a life of vision is right results. Your purpose becomes the key that opens the progress of the life you want to lead.

Every life succeeds by right purpose, and progresses by right decisions. In this world, so many lives have been damage because of things done aimlessly and haphazardly.

Right decisions and right choices must accompany your purpose. Purpose leads you to bear fruit. Right purpose bears right fruit, and bad purpose bears bad fruit.

Many people consider life as without rule and live it as they want; they never mind the outcome of such aimless living.

Aimless living becomes aimless life and ends in fruitlessness. Having a purpose in life makes a human being a human, and a life without purpose is already dead. Your decisions depend on your purpose. The Right purpose bears fruit based on positive thoughts and the bad purpose also bears fruit based on negative thoughts.

Your purpose shows the thought you have, and the life you live revolves around the thought you have.

A damaged life reflects the mindset of the person who lives such a life. Fruitful living shows the purpose of that life, and the banner of progress stands on rightful decisions. So many people live without thinking; they live aimlessly.

Every life needs a purpose and right decisions to get good rewards. Never live without the purpose.

Make sure, however, that you live with the right purpose, right decisions and right choices. Set the right goal, live by the right choices, watch your doings, and get ready for right rewards.

God will help you live by the right aim, good decisions, reasonable ends and great rewards for a better future. Think and think well.

You should not be narrow-minded; search for other opportunities and add up to what you already have. What do you have? What is your gift? What is your interest?

What do you always do? Ask yourself these questions and others. Then start with what you have little by little – do what you can about what you have.

Also, develop positive attitudes towards what you have and gradually multiply it little by little. You can never multiply your portion with idleness.

Invest time and resources into what you have. God has given human beings gifts, and these gifts are at your disposal too. Move by confidence with what you have given and appreciate it.

Having had your portion, you need to move confidently towards your goal. Your gift is your tool for daily living, and you are to account for it. Never joke with your gift.

God expects something big out. What you have – whether small or big – is what you deserve. Work with it, and it will bear fruit for your benefit and the benefit of others. It is then you will be regard as a good servant.

4. The Manager Considerations

Life is about considerations and the lessons which everyone must note. A good manager considered everything and manages to the best end. Today can be yours, but tomorrow will be someone else.

Everything concerns life is about eternal joy or doom. Never make merry without good and proper self-examination.

Take the life as yes or no principle, everything more than this is evil. Never demand what belongs to someone else's or withheld his or her rights.

Make no difference among men or women based on value the one than the other. Show respect to all people whether child; young or adult and cherish them. Do not show partiality in age among men or women but consider every age as due respect.

Be patient in all matters of life and be ready for good or bad. Plan correctly about the things you do and do the unique thing in the system and get the correct responses from the surrounding people.

Be prudent and act decency. Make Practice on good things and be kind to all people. Be ready to stand for truth and never deceive by your act; appearance or tongue.

Be alert to help and work from the correct heart. Work hard but not to abuse yourself, do away laziness and keep your time. Make peace with all men and do your part to promote justice.

Buy the truth but don't sell, share with others about what you know is the best and never cover what will benefit others.

Give as a hobby but never hoard up what benefit other, share the little and the big. Be diligent about your work and search for other avenues that promote life to it best.

Welcome people with a good approach and share your joy and sorrow. Be creative and do the best one day at a time. Be the servant to others in all the service to men but not as door mart.

Work as a master but act as a servant and be humble in all your doings. Be gentle but not too gentle; be forceful as law requires but not extending.

Life again consists of integrity; gentleness, forcefulness, preparation and good planning. We must be wise and as unwise depends on the condition not to cause damage to those who do not understand us.

Let's set good approach in all manners of life to promote humanity equality and to avoid differences. Let us show truelove to all people and fear God.

5. The Aim Life Penalties

A Life without a war is a life out of stage. So life with a war is the life of progress with aim.

Nobody can reach a high stage without a purpose coupled with industriousness and perseverance. God created everything in its perfect order. Why then has life become war every day? And why is a life difficult?

There are enemies of progress and these enemies are you, sin and the evil angel on your path every day. But, by the grace of God, You can be who you want to be, if you make Him king over you.

Every life starts with zero; true life depends on God for better fruits. Life offers a variety of lessons at every stage.

The lessons may come with happiness, tragedy, sorrow or mourning. All these are benefits of life because of the situations and conditions in which the world is.

Nobody in this world is without hope. But you cannot attain your aim in life unless you have a sense of purpose.

Life is sweet when you have what you need, and it is bitter when you lack your needs. Never grow weary in your pursuit; forge ahead to get it.

Your achievements lie on the ability to handle and utilise a purpose. You can handle your purpose by taking appropriate measures.

Nobody in this world can take it easy! I mean no one might achieve his or her needs without hard work.

So many people in this life want short-circuited lifestyle to enrich themselves. But that is dangerous, even when it becomes possible.

They end their lives suddenly. Be patient with whatever you want in life and with whatever you do. By patience and long suffering you will reach your destination.

You cannot go forward whilst you are still standing. Move and you will reach your destination by determination.

Be active in your movement and you will reach your stage. Do not slack or stop for any reason. Watch out on things that may cause you to slow down or stop. You are one out of a thousand; there is none like you.

See yourself as a unique person. What you have and your position differ from those of any other person. Appreciate what you have – even if it is a little – and guard it. Never lose hope but be grateful to God for what you have.

6. The Uncertain Life Impressions

When the life misses its rightful point, it behaves like the sea waves. When the life is uncertain in all points, it moves in directions whose control is difficult.

Sometimes, life becomes like walking in a muddy area; you do not know where to step. You are, sometimes, confused about deciding. It takes time for you to make a step in a muddy area. That's how life is. It takes patience to make a step forward.

Never let the life that seems like walking in the mud slow you down; move, never stand still. Make your direction anywhere you like and move ahead to get out from the mud you see.

Walking in the mud makes your movement slow; so is life. Life needs the patience to move along. Life is not like walking on an asphalt road where you can run or walk faster as you wish.

Life can silence you, like a dead lake. The faster you want it, the worse it becomes; the brighter you want it, the darker it becomes; and the sweet you want it, the bitter it becomes. But this is the qualification that life needs for its pure growth.

Never think it will be easy for you to step forward in life. It needs patience and carefulness. Many people want to get quick money and to enjoy luxurious cars and other pleasurable things. But what is the benefit of all these if you do not have Christ?

Life requires awareness, determination, truthfulness, proper planning and the help of God for success. Never let your hardship block your progress or prevent you from planning.

Try to build your house, regardless of the season. Take advantage of every situation you find yourself in; never give up. Life is how you want it to be and the condition in which you want yourself.

You cannot control everything life brings your way but you can own a better life by your willingness and attitude.

Life cannot entirely controlled but choice can win it. Better life is no respecter of age; it is a wish. Life must not stand still; it needs to pursue a wish – the reward for that life's choice.

Never think of the difficult circumstances you go through as a misery or a barrier to your progress; rather, let them motivate you to press on.

Bad wishes lead to bad choices and bad choices also lead to bad conditions. The condition of your wish leads to an expected outcome.

Plan to have a better condition so it will lead you to a better destiny. Life comprises negative and positive branches, and the fruit which it must bear to show the seed that was sown.

In life, the first seed one sows – whether good or bad – can be a mark that identifies the starting point of that life. A good foundation determines the strength of the whole building. Life well established brings hope for the future.

Every life starts with a struggle of a sort. Through that struggle the choice is made which brings your destiny.

Never leave God behind; never build life without Him. Never think that you can have a life of true peace by your own effort. A sea wave brings out something; so does a life of progress.

The human nature changes during the process of growth. In life, a change of situation brings maturity or immaturity depending on the choice that was made.

Every life needs to struggle. However, it must bear a fruit – or fruits – to reveal its identity. What struggle are you going through? You need to notice every stage of your life, because it is a lesson which will help you change your way of living.

The human life starts in the womb of a mother. The keys that initiate that life into success depend on the mother's action towards the baby in the womb.

Thus, the nature of a person's life depends partly on a mother's actions and inactions towards the baby during pregnancy.

Life's hardship mostly benefits us. But life's curses mostly depend on our mother's actions towards us. Mothers must, therefore, be careful about their actions towards their children.

Life is about actions and inactions. But life's prosperity stands on choices. Never be down-spirited because of hardship; be courageous and move forward.

All people may be against you but you will be successful in the end. The waves of life are inevitable. Sometimes, life can seem hopeless and dark as if you will not be successful. But be hopeful and courageous; never let it go.

Have faith in God and hold on to the end. Things will be better and profitable. Let your desire to succeed guide you to press even harder, when things are tough.

Discover what you need by searching deep. Discuss, work it out and hold on to the end. Never abuse your dignity or throw out your inner beauty because of your hard situation. Let your hope be in God, and be of good courage.

7. The Character Among Characters

A Life stands out for one particular thing – character. It is that which uniquely identifies a person.

Our character singles out each person and makes him or her real human being. Our life in this world thrives well on one thing – character. Our speeches, walks and actions make up our character.

People know you by your character; they love you by your character; and others hate you by your character.

People appreciate you by your character, come to you by your character, avoid you by your character, welcome you by your character, and reject you by your character. The only home of yours that people can identify is your character.

Character consists of the kind of behaviour we exhibit. It can determine our destiny forever. We need to watch out on our attitudes and behaviour each day.

The time offered us by God needs a careful consideration with our actions. The only fruit that God needs in his kingdom is our character. Good behaviour forms a good character which is a sign of good identity.

Our life's identity depends on a character. All is waste, if we gather all things and fail to gather good character. It is unnecessary.

You can become who you want to be. You can be a hero of all heroes, and you can be first in all things done on earth but your character must count more than all.

You cannot share your character but your character can let others know you. Never feign your appearance, because your character can reveal it to others.

You will lose your appearance when your real character comes out. Your name is your character and your character is your name. That is, your character will be your name in the coming days and that will determine where you should go.

What is your character? What character are you building? Some people's character identifies their face. Some strive for worldly properties but not a good character. Our character will be our name in heaven.

The only property that heaven needs is our character. God will not accept anything short of Him. Why do people worry themselves over things that profit nothing?

A good name is better than riches. That is, a good character is better than great wealth. Where are you focussing your life? Let me assure you that this world is not your home.

What is your decision? Where are you heading towards? What will be your next place of abode? Which destiny do you want? Your character today will choose your home tomorrow. Watch out!

8. The Abraham Faith and Trials

Who knows the beginning and the end results of life or who can predict the end result of every human being?

The world didn't come as the result of evolution as others unbelievers says, but it was planned and created by God (The Almighty).

The world we live is not like a vapour which appears and vanishes. It is a permanent plan, design and created for a purpose.

The things on this earth have purpose and activities. Why are you created or why are you in this earth today?

It is intentional for you to be on this earth. What do I mean? Your life was planned; design and made by God. This life has been subjected to two options. Who can tell the truth concerning people's life whether it will be good or bad?

It is not God purpose or never was his will to make us suffer; but it is a choice because of the freewill given to us. For I know the plans for I have for you, the plan for warfare and not for evil, to give you a future and a hope.

That is God's word for us. God purposely planned and design our life for specific used, and it is not by our will or by our decision to plan for our work in the future or in the set time.

Our work and the life journey has been design and proposed by God. That is, every person in this world has a skill or special gift for specific work to do.

So, it is not by chance or accident to be on this earth, you have the part to play. In fact, we were created as permanent beings with no death penalty. What transpire?

One thing that everyone must know is that, God needs your attention to play the best and to get the best reward!

Originally, man lost the idea of God and the aim in which he was created; because of the bad choice we made.

It is truth that God created us for specific work, but our free choice can make it void. Why because our nature today prefer the sin to the good.

In fact, God did not created dead being but the living beings. And it is God purpose for us to live as he is alive.

Sin has cost us the ceaseless death penalty. The whole world became dark through the sin of Adam and the world lost its beauty and the original state.

Furthermore, through God's love and kindness makes other way for us to be useful again. Let us consider this scripture;

Jeremiah 1:4-8

Now the word of the Lord came to me, saying, "Before I formed you in the womb I knew you, and before you were born I consecrated you; I appointed you a prophet to the nations.

"Then I said, "Ah, Lord God! Behold, I do not know how to speak, for I am only a youth. "But the Lord said to me,

"Do not say, 'I am only a youth'; for to all to whom I send you, you shall go, and whatever I command you, you shall speak. Do not be afraid of them, for I am with you to deliver you, declares the Lord."

This scripture testify the purpose of everyone been on this earth and the work set before him.

May be you do not know your skills or the work in which you are here to do. It is not your fault but it is a condition through the state the world has been now.

Then and again, you need lessons to study through this life stages; then finding the real job you have been created for. What do I mean and why Abraham faith and trials as a heading?

I wanted you to know more about yourself, and why you are here as a human being but not the other thing?

You have the work to do and it is your singular duty. This world is not there to walk in free but it is a fight.

To live is to fight and to fight is to live. Each one of us has a role to play, but it involves the test to purifying the life; then qualifies for the reward we are heading towards.

There is no name without the meaning and there is no hero without the test. You cannot be on the mountain top by escaping valleys, and you cannot be a hero without challenges. That is you need to pass through circumstances before, and then receive the reward.

Let's consider Abraham heroism and his victory in life. The man lost the contact of God and the way to the eternal life.

But God came to our aid and brought us back to himself through the call of the Abram (today's Abraham as we know).

This call benefits us again and paves the best contact. But Abraham did not take it easy as been a friend of God. Why and what is the purpose of the Abraham call?

Today many people want a cheap life but it cannot be or want to be hero in a short cut way but that is impossible.

Let's consider the way God led Abraham, and why God chose Abraham but not the other from his father's house? Who is Abraham and why God called him?

Abraham was the son of Terah, the Nahor's son. Nahor came from the Shem's family, the first born son of Noah. Abraham was brave; wise, calm, serious, meek but not weak. He was not blameless but childless. Why God called Abraham, the childless Man?

In this life, who can tell or predict the end results of someone's life? Abraham was the man like that, and there was no evidence you can stand on; and to tell something hope concerns the Abraham's life.

This man, Abraham doesn't know God as it should be, but he (Abraham) prepared himself to seek God.

Who can tell the end of the one who is hopeless in the sight of men? Are you in trouble that seems there is no way out?

Abraham and his wife were over age, and there wasn't any evidence concerning their life meaningful to have the son at their age.

But God took the meaningless thing to confound the meaning. Abraham did not give up concerning his situation; but firmly cope with and live on.

To be a hero is not joke, this life has many lessons that need to be study. You cannot wake up one day and say I am done.

Life and its best take long but it require patient to succeed. As the world and everything them was planned, designed and created, so as to our life purposely planned; design and created by God.

You have been designed by God to serve his purpose. You are the one that God knows not the other, your life is dear to him and he cannot leave you to struggle by your own effort!

It is not his will to suffer you wrong, but you need to be train and purify to look like him. Many people have seen you before, and they know your background and you are nobody to them, but God see you different.

Abraham was nobody at his time in sight of men but it wasn't so in the sight of God. Who know the beginning of the king?

God trained Abraham through circumstances, though he failed in some stage but he did not gave up. What it is about your life? Who knows? Every river source is very narrow but it ends in flood.

You are unique, you have what makes you, stand firm. The journey is long but you need to go with patient and take your reward. That is, rest not till you receive the crown! God have something best for you, note:

Now the Lord said to Abram, "Go from your country and your kindred and your father's house to the land that I will show you.

And I will make of you a great nation, and I will bless you and make your name great, so that you will be a blessing.

I will bless those who bless you, and him who dishonors you I will curse, and in you all the families of the earth shall be blessed."

Genesis 12:1-3.

9. The Jacob's Thought

Sometime many people decide or discuss on the short way to get wealth. Others find ways to get their future property today.

But how can a child be able to drive a car made for a man? Or how can you built a house without good foundation?

The life has stages and the manner it must be build. Never replace your life for empty wells but know the time and the stages you must go through.

Why the Jacob's thought? I want you to know more about the best life and the patience concerning that. Never aim what the world can measure, but aim what God could recognize or considered.

Do not be like Jacob in the matter of cheating the time, but be patient in all matters of the life stages. Note, do not force yourself to have the wealth that belongs to the other, and never cheat the time to get wealth.

Every human being has his or her stage to handle his or her wealth properly. Some take long time; other's a short time, others too hesitate; depend on the situation on how the life begins.

The world we are in was created by stages, each and every day has what was made by God, and the life we are in must go as the same. We need to have patient concerning every situation we are in.

There is the beginning and there is the end. Life has the beginning and the process it must pass through.

You cannot go before the time and you cannot go after the time; but you must go with the time. Everyone needs to keep the time but not to watch the time. Our life depends on daily activities and is also subjected to daily living.

Everyone have one day to live, and the daily living is subjected to the time and activities. Every time and hour is precious that makes the life value, but the misuse hours are the penalties of our future goal.

Everyone have one day to live and to harvest the eternal loss or gain. You cannot cheat the time and go free, but you will harvest the act fruit concerning that hour. What are all these comments?

We must live with faith and confidence in God and we should not fear to failed, but we must understand that it is part of the life.

God is faithful and he keeps his promise concerning our life. We need not rush in life but we need to have patient in life.

Though the life has become competition, but you need not to compete with anyone. You must wait and go with the time. Never ever rush as like Jacob, who desires to have his wealth before the set time and later on suffered.

Everyone needs to go with the time but not before the time or after the time. God has set eternity before us and we need to have patient and gradually go with the time. Everyone who rushes in the life lost the chance; dismantle the law and die before his or her time.

The heroes are not like that, but they manage and control their situation. They always wait and think before acting, and keep the time for the correct produce.

Every human being has the amount of wealth set up for him or her concerning his or her life.

The one who want more than require, ruin his or her life with many penalties. But those who want it as to the required enjoy the best of life and the peace of the rest of their time.

Every field has the color and the nature of that soil and the rivers has the dimension and the nature of it size. What do I mean? Everything has what it takes to make it whole.

The state of this world has the size and the volume or the amount that makes it reasonable. Everyone needs the sufficient in life to make the living reasonable.

Many people want to have more than the required for the life; and others demand more than the supply.

What do I want to say? Some people are very greedy; they want everything in life and even cheat others to have their wealth. What is life? And how must we live?

The world has the abundant, but it is not for the one man. Many people want to hoard up and even to destroy the rest.

This world has the demarcation as to the life we are in, and there are rights for everyone in birth and in life.

What it is for you is not for the other; and what it is for other is not for you. Never demand somebody's rights but manage yours; then protect your ability and destiny.

It took Jacob long time before overcoming his trials and depressions. He suffered because of covetousness of his brother's birth rights.

The true success in life is not earned by greediness; but earn by patient and the favor of God. Everyone who wants to live a worthy life needs patient and perseverance.

Those who take the life for granted suffered and destroy their destiny. You need patient in whatever you are doing; never rush in life, never go before or after the time, but with the time.

Do not destroy your gold or your wealth by haste or prolong your life success through greedy, but be thoughtful and manage the little you have.

Everyone have a life cycle and the process it must pass through. But the one who want to go beyond this process cause harm to his or her soul; and destroys the natural law.

God has designed each and everyone's life procedure and the age that meet his or her belongings.

You need to work and go through this process then make the life worthy and reasonable. Do not be like Jacob or thought like him at your age but wait for God's time, then fulfill your mission.

10. **Joseph Big Trouble**

The life has the matters and the way it must go, every human being has the secret about his or her life.

Our troubles today stands on the secret reveal to others about our life. Sometimes our life face many troubles not because of the secret revealed, but the progress it must suceed.

Though there are trials and trouble that the life needs to face to make the things right. But not all the troubles faced make things right. Some cause our doom forever and others waste our time for no improvement.

These troubles sometimes comes by our mistake or others too comes by our desire. Our death today was from the mistake made by our first parents.

In fact, life consist of happiness and sadness. There is no straight way for anyone to pass through concerning his or her life.

But every human being has the mystery about his or her life. That is the secret about his or her life and that secret needs to be carefuly keep and protect.

Joseph revealed the secret about his life to his brothers and that brought hatred to him.

You should not tell others or reveal to others what you have planned to do. But continue about what you want to do and proof to others what concerns you.

Some of our miserable state today stands on the secret reveal to others about our life. We need keep our mouth shut and manage whatever the condition we are in. The worlds we live have so many enemies fighting against our progress.

All nature is suffering because of sin and there is nothing that can cease these sufferings. But one thing we need to keep mind is that, we can cope with these sufferings by the help of God.

We have our part to do as human beings, though God can protect us excellently but we have bit play because of our free will.

Example was when Samuel was to anoint David as the king on Israel. God told Samuel not to let King Saul known what he was going to do.

Joseph trouble was to letting his brothers known his dream and this end him in Egypt with other troubles.

But he was able to overcome those trails through faith in God. Joseph passes through a lot of circumstances but he did not give up.

In this life, there are many troubles which everyone must face. Life cannot be straight as we want it to be, there will be happiness but we need to be careful on how we choose. We must be careful on how we say our words concerning our life.

This life is war always and it is up to us to know how to fight for our victory. In fact, we cannot do anything about it to cease from this fight. We need to keep our words well and manage every situation.

We need to shut up and make our words simple. Do not run after trouble or go before trouble but go with trouble and know how you will cope with it.

Whether you will go before or after trouble, you will still meet it. You need to go with and then manage it.

Otherwise, you will face what you cannot handle and fail. Sometimes these world troubles can help and make us strong. But it must come by correct channel; otherwise, we will fail and suffer than what expected.

In fact, we need to keep our secrets concerning the things about our life progress. Every good thing face trouble, we must keep a note. And again every good planning that makes life better; must be reserve secret.

Not all the things revealed to others, and not all the words revealed or say. Everyone must note this. Life conflicts comprise physical and spiritual; these two battles are real and can damage the life.

Never rush in life or do things for granted, you must be serious about the life and keep things in order. One mistake or one word uttered can cause your ruin.

The beginning of every life needs patience and how it must pass through. One way or the other, you must reach the goal. Means no matter the circumstance you must go forward.

Though life is difficult but you must fight and then achieve your goal. There are many difficulties but they all serve your progress.

Note difficulties are not temptations to destroy your life; but to set your life at liberty. But never take the life as easy as possible. Do not put your hope in anything but trust God.

Never rely on your ability or any knowledge you have but consider God first and move. You must keep yes or no principle to let God know your stand at each moment.

Do not boast or make merry at your victory, but give thanks to God and consider him each minute.

Never abuse your life because of late in progress. Do not be sad in trials or make a noise, but accept and move on. Joseph did not worry though he suffered but trusted God.

Maybe you are going through difficulties and it seems it is your mistake that has cause that. Things are not clear; hardly to understand what is going on in your life.

Do not be worry or sorry for yourself about your life; God understands, and it is his permission to save and to establish you well. You do not know what tomorrow will bring and you cannot predict what will be tomorrow.

Trust God and move, keep on your good works and manage the rest. What do you have? What are you doing now?

God will honor you according to what you have and what you are doing today in tomorrow. We will be promote or honor by what we are doing today.

Your life needs penalties to make it progress and you need to know and understand the life and it combats. Then make a prudent decision to better your lot. In fact, it is not your work to things favorable for you.

But is it your duty to fight and manage every difficulty to fulfill God's plan. Though, maybe you have revealed your secret to others as did Joseph and has ruined your life today.

Do not worry or feel sorry for yourself but have hope in God and trust him. As Joseph became king from prison, so you will be, by keeping on your integrity.

Do not be sad, who knows the king's life? Maybe you will be the rescuer for your whole family or the savior for your country in time of crisis.

Let's note:

Genesis 45:1-8

Then Joseph could not control himself before all those who stood by him. He cried, "Make everyone go out from me.

" So no one stayed with him when Joseph made himself known to his brothers. And he wept aloud, so that the Egyptians heard it, and the household of Pharaoh heard it.

And Joseph said to his brothers, "I am Joseph! Is my father still alive?" But his brothers could not answer him, for they were dismayed at his presence.

So Joseph said to his brothers, "Come near to me, please." And they came near. And he said, "I am your brother, Joseph, whom you sold into Egypt.

And now do not be distressed or angry with yourselves because you sold me here, for God sent me before you to preserve life.

For the famine has been in the land these two years, and there are yet five years in which there will be neither plowing nor harvest.

And God sent me before you to preserve for you a remnant on earth, and to keep alive for you many survivors. So it was not you who sent me here, but God. He has made me a father to Pharaoh, and lord of all his house and ruler over all the land of Egypt.

11. The wrong Act Consideration (Moses)

Sometimes God consider our negative act that wishes to save someone's life in a certain condition. But not that God support it, but the way it was acted to save the life.

Our act have a lot to do, every human being is known by his act. The life itself consist of act or doing, there can be no life without act. Every act proceed count a lot and without act, there is no life. One thing that everyone must know or note is the way we act.

God consider every act proceeded out. Human beings are known by their act but the result makes the identity.

Moses does not know that his act was considered being a leader. Any act we proceed dertermine our stand whether good or bad. Let consider this scripture;

Exodus 2: 11- 15

One day, when Moses had grown up, he went out to his people and looked on their burdens, and he saw an Egyptian beating a Hebrew, one of his people. He looked this way and that and seeing no one; he struck down the Egyptian and hid him in the sand.

When he went out the next day, behold, two Hebrew were struggling together. And he said to the man in the wrong, "Why do you strike your companion?"

He answered, "Who made you a prince and a judge over us? Do you mean to kill me as you killed the Egyptian?"

Then Moses was afraid, and thought, "Surely the thing is known." When Pharaoh heard of it, he sought to kill Moses. But Moses fled from Pharaoh and stayed in the land of Midian. And he sat down by a well.

Our acts are always considered by God and the manner in which it was acted is weigh and carried. God considers any act that no matter the background or the negative it is.

Another thing we need to consider about our acts is that, those acts precede can leads to our future goal or work. Every practice has the future harvest and the fruit that generates.

The children are known by their acts and that act most determines their future work whether negative or positive makes their future goal.

Every human being has his or her part to play in this life or acts. Your today acts can lead to your future goal. What do I mean concerning these comments?

In this life, every act shows the future destiny. What you will determine today or think of today can fulfil in tomorrow's life.

Your beautiful life today can be miserable tomorrow. Any thoughts concerning any act leads to eternal death or eternal life.

The One way or the other, everyone needs to think and make the right decision. And another thing, we need to note is that God's way is not as the human being thinks. Your life has the biography written by God and there is no way anyone can change it. But any performance contrary to the law of God; can dismantle the beauty of that biography.

Means you can destroy your life by your wrong act and makes the different about your destiny. Men never ever joke of every dot; jot or comma of any act; it can set your life aim without remedy.

Sometimes your thought set the life into no return point. And sometimes too makes you prosper on the way you act towards it. Every good act negatively perform can be recognized by God to earn the best result.

Let everyone act to save the other's life; then saves their life too. Your thought can lead you to life eternal and to eternal death. Moses act shown his thought and led him the leader of Israel. He couldn't imagine that such the act God recognized him.

Your good works negatively performed to save the life has been valued by God. Though you did it negatively but heaven have made it reasonable.

Does God support Moses murdering? No but he considered to be good practice, but he (Moses) did it wrong way.

God consider every good work may be performed wrongly. That is why no man can boast of his good works or justify by his good works, but by faith.

God accept us in all matters of life and consider our will of making a good choice; but justify us by faith not by our good works.

You can be the leader of God's people like Moses; and can be somebody that the world known as a hero. But you cannot be credited by your good works in heaven.

God recognized us through our wish or will emerge into his will and accept us as we are. No matter our condition as sinful beings, we are always welcome by God. This world is totally doomed and damage by sin, but there is a way out.

Israel of old was a servant to Pharaoh and there wasn't any hope of relief from that slavery.

May be you are like that today, sin have shut you into the bottomless pit; to you there is no way of escape, you have lose hope and you do not know what to do?

Remember the one who created the heavens and earth; He knows you and remembers you.

Though may be your life has become dark today, and you have been discourage by the surrounding waves. Oh my dear, God is preparing Moses to come to your aim and free you forever.

You can be somebody tomorrow and you can hero. But you need to act in the manner of practicing a good choice.

God is always seeking to find out a sinner who will accept him as his creator and savior. Who knows the result of his or her act?

May be your good wish wrongly performed can set you free forever and be like Moses tomorrow. You need to determine and makes the different of your life today to exchange your wreck tomorrow. Note this scripture:

Hebrews 11:23-28

By faith Moses, when he was born, was hidden for three months by his parents, because they saw that the child was beautiful, and they were not afraid of the king's edict.

By faith Moses, when he was grown up, refused to be called the son of Pharaoh's daughter, choosing rather to be mistreated with the people of God than to enjoy the fleeting pleasures of sin.

He considered the reproach of Christ greater wealth than the treasures of Egypt, for he was looking to the reward.

By faith he left Egypt, not being afraid of the anger of the king, for he endured as seeing him who is invisible. By faith he kept the Passover and sprinkled the blood, so that the Destroyer of the firstborn might not touch them.

12. **King but a servant (David)**

Can the dry ground be planted or can the desert spring up with river? Who knows the end of a servant?

Is it possible for the servant to become king? Do royals can be overthrown? Is there any hope for the destitute?

In fact, this world has a lot of lessons that needs to be study. And again there are histories that need to be reconsidering again.

Many people consider weeds instead of seed; others consider sand instead of gold, and others admire giants instead of intelligent.

Many other people prefer fake instead of the original. Some also seek for beauty without quality and so on. What do I mean? Many people in the world always look at the surface and never mind the interior.

Others prefer beautiful giants without intelligence. Some also admire body instead of ability and the wise. There are many people who always consider empty bottles as a substitute for fill bottles.

It is not all that shine is the light to prevent darkness. And gain not all sand is use for building a house; and not all soil is good for planted the seed.

Those who are wise and able to do are sometimes regardless by men because of their form or state. Others are rejected because of their poverty.

But the world cannot move to it best without these people who are less regarded. Some people are nothing before their family, but they are the ones who hold the key to the success.

Their stature is not welcome, or it is not what you will desire, but they are truly heroes among men.

These people are able and intelligent. They are like termites you cannot value them, but they built tomes of houses and skyrockets.

They are industries, wise and practical. There are many wonders in the world; some of these wonders are not esteem by people because their state. Let us consider some of these wonders less regard in nature.

Proverbs 30:24-28

Four things on earth are small, but they are exceedingly wise: the ants are a people not strong, yet they provide their food in the summer; the rock badgers are a people not mighty, yet they make their homes in the cliffs; the locusts have no king, yet all of them march in rank; the lizard you can take in your hands, yet it is in kings' palaces.

Do not look and measure men at your own eyes but weigh by their ability and again do not compare; because they all have their stand.

May be you are nothing before your family; nothing before your country, nothing before colleagues, because of your poverty and stature.

But God remembers you; you are somebody and admire by God. Do not be discourage because of your poverty or your state which seems without hope.

King David was like that, his family rejected him, and he was less esteemed but intelligent and admire by God.

People respect giants without good attitude; they admire weeds instead of seed; they love quantity instead of quality.

Some also respect those of big titles but inactivity. In this world, people with hope are impractical but people without hope are useful. Never discriminate and look down on others.

Do not measure men with your eye and value the one than the other; but respect each and know that, they all have their stand and value.

Do not be deceived by big giant bodies or control by charm things. There are many people who are not as you measure or value.

Some are flesh without bones and other's bones without flesh. That is, they look attractive but they are measureless. Let us note this scripture;

1samuel 16:6-13

When they came, he looked on Eliab and thought, "Surely the Lord's anointed is before him." But the Lord said to Samuel, "Do not look on his appearance or on the height of his stature, because I have rejected him.

For the Lord sees not as man sees: man looks on the outward appearance, but the Lord looks on the heart." Then Jesse called Abinadab and made him pass before Samuel. And he said, "Neither has the Lord chosen this one."

Then Jesse made Shammah pass by. And he said, "Neither has the Lord chosen this one." And Jesse made seven of his sons pass before Samuel.

And Samuel said to Jesse, "The Lord has not chosen these." Then Samuel said to Jesse, "Are all your sons here?" And he said, "There remains yet the youngest, but behold, he is keeping the sheep." And Samuel said to Jesse, "Send and get him, for we will not sit down till he comes here." And he sent and brought him in. Now he was ruddy and had beautiful eyes and was handsome.

And the Lord said, "Arise, anoint him, for this is he." Then Samuel took the horn of oil and anointed him in the midst of his brothers.

And the Spirit of the Lord rushed upon David from that day forward. The world we live has misunderstandings; not what the world valued is valuable before God.

Do not think that one deserve than the other who you value because of the height or the beauty.

Never again think that the poor in stature in your own estimate have nothing to serve. But they are the ones who carried water among men and able as an ant.

This book title (The Hero's Track) is pointing to the people who are ready to fight the good fight of faith, and are ready to stand faithfully no matter the trials.

The heroes are the people who stand no matter the circumstance or the conditions hardly to entertain.

They never think of big names; wealth or anything worthy but they look before God and admit their condition whether good or bad; but believing that, they will have their good reward on earth and the world to come.

Never laugh at the poor in stature or disregard the man who is the youngest in life. Who knows the life of a king?

13. Ideas but lack of means

It is sad to be poor whiles you have knowledge which can benefit entire world. Many people have ideals which can help their life and others but poverty has shut them down.

Lack of means makes life stand still and makes ideals meaningless. In fact, life without means makes no improvement. No matter how great your knowledge will be, without means you cannot improve.

Though ideals increase means but without means ideals will be fruitless. Many people have ideals but lack means for it improvement. Life of a man depends on means and ideals for better improvement physically.

Knowledge increment is built by means. In order words, there will be no development without means and knowledge been apply.

Also, means without knowledge or ideals will flop; no matter how that person is mature in age or not.

So, means without knowledge cannot be prospered. These two gifts are very important for the growth of human beings.

So, when someone have ideals and does not have means, there will be no proper development. Here the peak poor man as the title of this book is the lesson of a certain man who became so poor for the lack of means.

The man has ideals alright but lack means to make things better for his and others. He became poor for the lack of means. What brought his poverty?

He was born by a poor woman and the father who does not care. So, the man could not complete school. He was a dropout student by lack of funds.

He tried to work for his own, that is he was a self-employ person. The work he chose was not suited his carrier as he wish it to be. But he continued to do it for the time being.

Thinking that, it will be better for some time. But it keeps on the same as from the beginning. He wasn't give up but stand firm for some years. He tried to find ways and means to makes his life dear but it keeps on the same.

In life, sometimes you will think as you has been curse by someone but it is not so. You do not know the ways of God.

In all, the man did not give up or be discouraged by his situation. He has great ideals when you listen to him through his speech.

You cannot understand why is it so in others life? What makes his poverty so great is that, he has ideals to create job; that is he is a business minded person, but lack of means delayed his ability to do that.

This man spent about 65 percent of his years before covered as a great philosopher.

What do I want us to lesson and share? Means and ideals are friends for which the absences of one will make the other fruitless.

We all need to watch out and observe things together. Someone's knowledge is a food for somebody.

Another one's income is aid for improvement of ideals and betterment of all people. Let us all help to improve of our lives by means of sharing the ideals and means together for our own advancement.

Ideals but lack of means; makes life bitter and abysmal to the one who is in such condition, and then kills those who lack both, which he will be a benefit to them.

Let those who have means seek and help those who have ideals but lack means for the improvement of the whole city.

Ideals but lack of means has made many people useless in societies. Many talents have been buried for the lack of funds.

It is your duty and my duty to help people to succeed by helping them with the tittle knowledge and means we have for the betterment of people.

Do not keep your means for selfish use but give and let others survive by your means. You who have an ideal must share for the progress of all people.

One knowledge or ideal shared can create jobs for thousands of people who are jobless.

Your little income freely given can increase employment for the society in which you live.

Do not let someone die through your selfishness. Share and let us all multiply and improve for your own blessings and then live and die in peace. We shall all go and it will not leave a bird.

14. Knowledgeable but less recognition

Poor has no friend and have no place among the kings. How can a tree on the desert be valued? Who will like to live on the desert? Can a servant be recognized by the prince?

Who likes to sit on the heat of sun? Who will bath on the dead lake instead of live lake? We all love sweet than bitter and love fame than ordinary.

Knowledge with poverty is like a bank of cloud without water. You shall be seen but with no recognition.

It is all because of your poverty. You cannot be remembered among congregation of your church and your name will be forgotten by the people around you.

It is because of your poverty. You can save the entire world through your knowledge, but your poverty will let men take you for granted. Why because you do not have money? Your name will be lost because of your poverty.

Knowledgeable but less recognition is the lack of means for proper growth and recognition in the world.

Poor do not have name and those who are in poverty cannot be select to be a leader in the church or a country, no matter your knowledge or ideals. People will reject you by means of your poverty.

This is the world we live which is difficult for a poor person to be a leader. It is not possible from east to west, south and north. Only God can make it possible for a poor to be a leader.

Your poverty can let child step on you, no matter your ability or skills. Poor have no associate among the society. You can build to the top but you will not be recognizing because of your paucity of means.

You can imagine those who have names in the world. Are they poor? People in the world are not fair, you know why?

They can erect wicked to rule them, instead of knowledgeable and God fearing. It is because of money. In this world, money rules but not knowledge.

A pampered person can lead wise men because of his money or wealth. Your ideals cannot be a benefit to people unless you have wealth or money.

Else you shall go to grave without benefiting anyone with your ideals. People love money than knowledge and love pampered with money than wise counsel.

It is difficult for a poor to a king or queen in his or her hometown with all the ideals that person have. People do not care even if it left you on the royal line; then there will be no king or queen because of your poverty.

They will go for a servant who is richer than you as their king but not you. It does not matter your knowledge or skills, they will choose the illiterate with money.

This is the world that we live, it takes God for a poor to be a leader for the nation or church. So it is profitable, to be a knowledgeable person with wealthy and God fearing.

Then you shall be a king among kings and the leader among leaders. Poor has no friend and they are less recognize in the city no matter their ideals, money count.

It is a fact that money instruct than knowledge and rich men lead than poverty. You cannot be recognizing, unless you have money. This is the world we live; money governs but not knowledge.

15. Be Active and do away poverty

Can you imagine how bitter it is when poor person want to do something with no means to begin? What can you compare? It is like walking in the muddy area and at the same time raining.

This is tragedy and horrible. To be poor means to be buried alive with no mercy. Poverty makes life bitter and dangerous. It can leave you fear and lack of hearing.

A poor person who is active becomes inactive through his poverty. Who can tell or explain this situation? In life whatever a person does improve his or ability. But what it means when you are poor?

This poor man as I am writing about him was very active and serious but poverty made him inactive in the sight of men who around him. It came a time he was sacked from the room he rented by his landlord.

It wasn't easy for his life. Oh who can understand the burden of the poor man and understand the state of his burden? Life cannot be a life unless it bears fruit.

Not just a fruit but the fruit of honesty and modest. Your activeness in life cannot be fruitful without means and knowledge.

In fact, it is difficult to come out from pit that contain muddy on it bottom without ladder to assist you to come out. The degree that is earned in the school of poverty is desperation.

Poverty can close your ears and eyes that foreseen ahead. It can leave you forgetfulness when you are not careful.

It can change the way you walk; talk and dress. You become useless a man or woman because of poverty. It shut you from events and opportunities.

Poverty can dress you up and give you a name. It always gives you pressure and inner talk. It is a disease that does not have remedy. It is only God who can heal this kind of nature.

Never thought it is your strength that made you rich. It is not so. Who can straight what God has curved? Poverty is gift which help people to know more about human sufferings.

It is not a curse but a situation that everyone needs taste in his or her life sometime. It helps you to depend on God deeply.

Then helps you realizes that you cannot do anything without Christ. Poverty also help built our hope in God. But poverty without Christ is doom.

No one should entertain it. When you are active but poor do not give up; do your best as you can. Keep in mind that poverty does not come by laziness. But if you wish to be lazy then you become poor.

Such people should not be entertained and my writing of this book is not for lazy people who have become poor through laziness.

This book is for those who are naturally poor by God's grace and willing to come out with their best effort.

If you are active but poor do not give up. You must be faithful to the end. But do not blame God for your poverty. It is for your good and great expectation.

Be active to the end and turn things round. It shall be well. It shall be well. Here are my main content comments. The peak poor man and now billionaire as the title of this book concerns you read this book.

Do you want to be in the same situation you are in now? It is better or best or not? Do you wish to stay where you are now and forever? What can you do to change your life that suits enough?

What is your work? It is good or not? What income do you get or earn from the work you are doing now? Are you a teacher? Are you a doctor or any other works professionals?

What have you thought off concerning your work today? Do you want to expand it or add one or two? Your life has no limit to earn other things for good and others benefits.

Means you have ways and means to do more when you have life. Do not think it is okay and there is no need to add another value yourself. How can you become a billionaire?

Do government workers are billionaires? Do you know someone who is government worker and a billionaire? Is it not possible? Unless that person steals or be a business man on a setting firm owner, it is not possible.

You need to add another value to yourself. That is, change your style of living and change your job.

Billionaires are creative and thinkers and work for their own. That is, they are owners of business firms and into other productions. You can change your situation by changing your mind on how you think.

It is impossible to come out from your pit without ladder. That is, you need to think ahead and plan well about your life. If you aim high, you will earn high.

You should not be a narrow minded but think broadly and live on the narrow path. Means be faithful in your work and work diligently but not as a cheater.

On this way, you will be a billionaire and have rest for your soul. Do not cheat to earn money but work with your hands and be honest. Through your faithfulness, you will earn your means without stress.

The peak poor man and now billionaire as this book title; is letting us to know how to behave towards your work and correct way of making a good choice of work that benefit you and others for fame.

It is not possible for a poor man to live comfort in terms of goods. It is possible for rich men to have what they need.

How you consider this tricky lesson message have and what do you want to do now about your state? Do something and change your style of living and think trice.

Learn to live well and learn to add value to yourself. Water your farm in the morning and evening. That is, continue doing what you have started and do another thing that suits the first one.

It is not late; you can do something again and again. Do not cease until you die. But do your best and be honest. Do not be lazy and sleepwalker.

Be strong and courageous never let it go until you have done the peak and the best equal to your strength.

You can be a billionaire, if you change style of think to your work. It is not late at all. Consider the way you think and behave towards your work well.

That is, be a diligent worker and do honest work wherever you are. God will consider you and then build you up.

Be active and do away poverty through the little you have and have positive mind towards your doings.

16. What makes you different?

It is not all the birds that sing the sweet song but there is a bird which sings a song for moves or dancing. What do I mean? There is something that makes differences between people.

We all have identities and characters. Here, everyone must come out with something that makes his or her name. It is difficult to identify a person without his or her activities. But the difference comes from acts or behaviour.

It is not your words that makes the difference but your actions. Your words are your witness but your act is your security. In fact, you cannot be famous unless you act accordingly.

It is not just a word but the behaviour. What is your goal? Where do you focus? What do you want to do? Many people have failed because of selfishness. Others have been broken because of greedy.

What have you planned to do? Life is how you want it but fame is an act of action you have made. You need to do something that supersedes what others have done.

The difference is the name you will get at the end. Do you cheat others by your power? What makes you different? Each one of us must have something unique that identifies his or her personality.

Actions and words of a person make his or her character. But attitude answers the results. In fact, our life on this earth has shortened and it is not God's wish at the beginning.

But whatever your life, it must impact on people for good. That is, you must do something exceptional for recognition. What have you done for your recognition?

It is not your wealth that makes you exceptional but your attitude. There are many things that form our attitude; dresses, speech, walk and the others.

All these make a person and the identity of each individual. What character are you forming? Whatever you do form your identity or character.

There are a lot for us to do as human beings. Everyone must do something that will serve as an example for others to benefit from it.

It is not what you do but what you do from the love that matters. We always sometimes want to do things that will let others know our fame but does not do things that will let others recognize our goodness.

Your greatness does not come by your words but it comes by your act of love that makes another benefit. So, it is time for you to do something that will make you a good name forever.

You must speak differently; see differently, dress differently, sing differently, eat differently and then act differently. But it must impact for good but not for evil.

You must be different altogether from all people; in your actions, in your dress, in speech and your walk.

In fact, your life must be different from others. You must live differently from others. You must have different faith and character.

You must be exceptional from others. You must see differently from whatever others see. Be unique and prudent in all matters of life. You need to do something that will make you different altogether.

You must leave a legacy to your children's children. You haven't done anything yet. You must do something and then make a good account of your life.

You should not depend on the opinions of others to live your life, but you must decide for yourself and live uniquely. You must learn and teach at the same time, but you must be unlike others. You must do things appropriate than the others. Make difference between right and wrong; clean and unclean. You must show dignity and knowledge in all your doings.

Try to do things well and then makes a difference in your appearance. You must welcome others with good approach and decency.

Let the world consider your legacy and your fame that have a good name and glorify God about it.

What makes you different? Have you done something that others will benefit from it? In all, do the right thing and then let others learn from it. They all looking at you, what are you leaving for them?

For Good Living and Knowledge Gain!
B. B. S. LIFE BOOKS.

The Hero's Brave Decisions

Also by Bernard Benson Sarfo

The Fact Among Facts (1st)
The Fact Among Facts

Standalone
The Youth Murderer
Be Original Not a Copy
The Christians Science or Scholarship
Precious than Paradise
Habit makes future
A shelter from storm and rain
The Science of Life
The Strongest Lion Knockback
The Perfect and Inspiring City
Above Hope, Faith and Love
The Hero's Brave Decisions
The Weakest Among Plants
The Hero's Brave Decisions

About the Author

Bernard Benson Sarfo is an acquainted architectural designer and a motivational speaker.He is a gifted teacher who continues to motivate and encourage many.

Read more at https://www.amazon.com//author/bbslifebooks.

www.ingramcontent.com/pod-product-compliance
Lightning Source LLC
Chambersburg PA
CBHW021801150726
47989CB00004B/1751